Copyright © 2017 by Pro English Writers

All rights reserved. No part of this publication may be reproduced or transmitted in any form, whether electronic or mechanical, including photocopying, recording, or sharing without the expressed written permission from the publisher.

Disclaimer. The information contained in this book, as well as the website referred to herein, are meant to serve as a collection of proven strategies that the author of this book has applied for financial gain. The information contained in these pages are solely recommendations by the author, and reading this book does not guarantee that one's results will mirror the results described herein. The author of this book has made all reasonable effort to provide current and accurate information. The author will not be held liable for any unintentional errors or omissions that may be found or inferred herein.

www.proenglishwriters.com

Acknowledgements

This book is the collective effort of the entire Pro English Writers' team. While only one author gets listed on the cover, the hundreds of hours logged by team members have been critical to the creation of this book, and highly appreciated.

Table of Contents

Chapter	Content
1	Improving your writing
2	Introduction
3	Benefits of SEO Writing
4	Terminology
5	8 Essential Components to SEO Writing
6	A Writing System that Works
7	Build Your Portfolio
8	Conclusion
Appendix	7 Tips for Writing Amazing English Essays

Chapter 1

Improve Your Writing- Exchanging Your Time for Our Time!

The focus of this book is to present an opportunity to improve your writing skills. This book outlines the opportunity for you to access the Pro English Writers' team of experts. And the best part? You will have access to our team for free. That's right- this book outlines the opportunity for you to exchange your time (not your money) for our time (not our money).

SEO writing presents a wonderful opportunity to improve your writing skills, while earning money in the process. However, it will take a while before you begin earning money through SEO writing. You will need to build your online portfolio (which is much like an online résumé), as well as develop some basic skills before clients will begin paying you to write. These skills are developed through writing and use. Pro English Writers will be your partner in this endeavor, and we will provide you the opportunity to publish your work, and thus, build your portfolio. And we will provide feedback and tips on how you can improve your writing. Sound amazing? Well, it should!

The purpose of this book is to provide you (the author) and Pro English Writers (the authority) the opportunity to mutually benefit. As the author, you will receive writing practice and free feedback from the Pro English Writers' team of experts for developing your writing skills. You will be introduced to a viable option of earning income in the long term, and you can even start building your online portfolio with our help along the way. Pro English Writers is able to offer our services in editing your writing for free through publishing your articles online on our web site. In this way, we are both able to exchange our time, without having to exchange any money in the process of helping each other- this arrangement is strictly time for time; no money will be earned from your initial writing projects in building up your own writing portfolio. Sound too good to be true? It gets even better!

For many of you, taking these skills to the next step of actually earning money to write will be an exciting proposition. Imagine that after developing your writing skills, and building up your online portfolio, that you can actually get paid to write. That's right- get paid for writing the kind of articles that we would have written and polished together already. This book will briefly outline ways of establishing an SEO writing income, and occasionally, Pro English Writers will even bring SEO writers onboard. That's right, we will hire exceptional writers that prove their abilities through the process described above (writing practice articles, editing practice articles, and publishing the articles on our web site).

Chapter 2

Introduction

This book provides an overview of SEO writing. While there are parts of this book that touch on the business side of this opportunity, the primary purpose is to educate you on what is possible through SEO writing. We are not attempting to provide you a lock-and-key method for establishing an SEO company in this book. There are plenty of resources available on the web that can fill this need. We will take a focused approach in helping develop your skills throughout this book, for the benefit of all readers who are not looking for any business details.

In order to get started in SEO writing, there are only a few basic requirements. You will need access to a computer (desktop or laptop), internet (preferably high speed), basic ability to write in English, and the ability to use Google to find information. Of these four requirements, the writing ability in English may seem the most intimidating. The required writing skills for SEO writing is being able to produce a functional article, virtually error-free. So don't worry- being able to produce amazing content with your own unique style, while indicative of higher quality work, is not a requirement for basic SEO writing.

SEO stands for search engine optimization. SEO writing is a form of writing that help websites become more prominent in major search engines such as Google and Bing. Basically, SEO writing involves providing content to web sites, which draws visitors to the site from Google. When you enter information into Google, a number of search results get provided by Google. Out of the millions of web sites out there, Google chooses a page of results for the individual web surfer to view. These select websites receive lots of visitors as a result of Google directing web surfers to their websites. This is the purpose of SEO writing- to have Google rank web sites highly, enabling web sites to receive some of the incredible amounts of web traffic that Google directs to different web sites every minute of every single day.

A typical SEO writing job will involve four key steps. The first requires research concerning the keywords that a website wishes to rank highly for. For example, Apple would wish to have visitors directed to their website who are searching for information regarding electronics, not cars! Determining keywords is most often provided by clients and involves determining what kind of person a web site is looking to attract (e.g., someone who is searching online for information concerning household goods). Secondly, once the keyword is determined, the next step is to decide relevant content. A quick search using Google can provide you with infinite information on any topic. Third, content is written centering around the keyword.

Finally, other people read your article and share your work on Facebook, Twitter, and other social media platforms.

Generally, a client will provide a topic (such as 'the best way to lose 5 kilos in one week' or 'the best sources of omega-3 essential fatty acids'), and a keyword, and your job will be to research the topic and write an original article on the topic. When people search Google for specific information, the words that are entered into Google are known as keywords. For a website, keywords are those specific targeted areas that a web site hopes to gain traffic directed by Google. Therefore, a web site owner will pay for an article that will help the website's chances of appearing on the first page of Google search results for that keyword. The importance of a keyword for an SEO writer is to simply ensure that your article contains that keyword a couple of times in the article. That's basically it for keywords, though we will discuss keywords in greater detail in chapter 4.

A typical SEO writing project will consist of a 500-700 word article. Basic research makes this easy. Simply enter the keyword or topic into Google, and use the search results to find plenty of useful information. Be sure to not copy and paste anything you find! This is plagiarism, and guarantees that clients will not pay you for your 'work.' With experience, you will develop your own system for obtaining information for your article (e.g., how many web sites you consult, how many pages of written notes you collect), but I recommend checking at least 5 web sites for your first few articles. Take notes of the useful information you find as you inspect each web site, and develop an outline that is thorough enough to complete your 700 word article. While you are learning the ropes, take your time and be sure to not cut corners in gathering potential ideas for your article.

Articles must be your original work. Google not only rewards quality, original content, but also penalizes web sites that contain duplicate content. All clients demand original content, and there are many easy methods to check for plagiarism and duplicate content. So rather than risk your reputation and burning bridges with clients, ensure that you provide quality, original content.

Chapter 3

Benefits of SEO Writing

In order for you to properly assess the viability of this opportunity for reaching your professional and financial goals, we will outline the main advantages below. Keep in mind that this list presents the advantages of getting involved in SEO writing. As with all opportunities, there are challenges as well; namely, this endeavor requires patience and hard work. It will be challenging to establish a writing income that meets your financial and professional goals. It will take time. However, everything in life requires overcoming obstacles, and the benefits below should help you determine whether this business opportunity is worth the time and effort for you.

Benefit 1 – Lack of Competition

SEO writing is largely unknown. Don't believe me? Ask your friends, colleagues, and those you consider worldly to describe to you what exactly SEO writing is. There is a very good chance that this exercise will validate the fact that most people are largely unaware about the SEO writing opportunities that are available.

With global English writing needs on the upswing in general, and the proliferation of new web sites coming online daily, the lack of awareness surrounding SEO writing plays to your benefit. A lack of awareness equates to lower levels of competition. A market with lower competition provides you market power- the ability to set price levels, and acquire new contracts. Being able to establish yourself in a relatively unknown, but growing, market represents an ideal opportunity offering unlimited potential.

Benefit 2- Freedom

SEO writing provides you the freedom to dictate your life. This flexibility allows you to work as much, or as little, as possible depending on your own personal circumstances. If you need to pay off debt, such as a mortgage or a flashy new purchase, spend extra hours working and earning income in order to meet your needs. If you need more free time due to family obligations, such as the birth of a new child, then cut back on your workload accordingly. Time is the world's most valuable commodity, and SEO writing allows you to maximize this priceless resource.

In addition, SEO writing does not require any expensive or fancy uniform. Without a doubt, hours of ironing eliminated from not having to dress in a suit or company uniform will not be missed. Neither will the drycleaning bills for those delicate garments. You choose your work attire, or lack thereof, and give up trying to impress your officemates.

Benefit 3- Easy to learn

You may consider yourself a poor writer. This is probably due to your failed attempts in school of producing an essay that impressed your teacher. The truth is that SEO writing involves a specific system of writing rather than a comprehensive vocabulary list or complex sentence structures. This system can- and will- be easily learned. We will outline all the required parts in the next chapter.

Benefit 4- Low Barriers to Entry

Many businesses require large upfront capital costs, advanced skills in order to succeed, and extensive marketing campaigns. One major advantage to SEO writing is that you do not need any of these in order to become successful.

There are very few obstacles for getting started. On the technology side, all you need is a computer, internet, email account, and paypal account. You may choose long term to develop a website for promoting your talents, but this is not required. In addition to the technological requirements, you need time available for performing SEO writing tasks, the ability to learn information about a wide variety of topics as required, and the ability to type your work in English.

If you lack any of the above requirements, do not worry. These are all things that can be met with a little time and energy. Sign up for an email account or paypal account now. Practice typing to increase your skills and speed. Join our mailing list (https://proenglishwriters.com/tips/) for ways to develop your English writing skills.

Benefit 5- High Earnings Potential

Starting off in SEO writing offers you the ability to earn $10-15 per 500-700 word article. This is not going to get you rich anytime soon, but it represents a decent income while you are developing your writing skills. I'd be surprised if any reader cannot earn more than the minimum wage offered in your specific country of origin using the basic pay rate above. Even one article per hour, which is not overly ambitious in the medium term, affords an income of $10-15 per hour. All the while you are being paid to develop your skills and investing time in building your future. Every job you finish (and earn approximately $10-15 in the process) is helping you build your skills and your speed of doing SEO writing jobs. Wow- sign me up!

But of course the earnings above will not motivate many to get involved in SEO writing for the long term. However, I have good news for you: As your skills improve, and you build your online writing portfolio, doors will open for you to earn much more. First of all, the required time to complete the basic entry-level SEO writing jobs described above will vastly decrease. You will figure out tricks and methods to cut the time required to complete SEO writing jobs. This may include faster typing speed, more efficient research methods, more efficient writing ability, and increased general knowledge.

In addition, there are many higher-end SEO writing jobs out there. You can contact businesses directly and offer your SEO writing services to website or business owners. Or you can write guest blogs or posts for various web sites and earn $100 or more per article. There are many web sites that pay these rates for quality writing, usually between 700-1500 words (on the next page you will find a few sample web sites) . As you might expect, the quality demanded of these higher paying writing jobs is often significantly higher than the standards for basic SEO writing jobs.

Here are 11 web sites offering paid writing work:

General Web Sites

Listverse

$100

Blessthislist

$100

Dissent Newswire

$100-250

Salon

$100-200

Finance

The Money Pantry

up to $150

Ecommerce Insiders

$125

Parenting

Fine Parent

$100-200

Metro Parent

$35-350

Travel

Transitions Abroad

up to $150

The Travel Writer's Life

$150-200

International Living

$250- 400

There are numerous paths that become available once you have mastered the skills required for SEO writing. Starting off in SEO writing, which is the focus of this book, takes time in order to develop skills and confidence prior to targeting the jobs listed in the chart on the previous page. However, the long-term focus is worth mentioning here as you embark on your SEO writing journey.

Chapter 4

Terminology

Every industry has its own terminology that describes the relevant characteristics or processes that make it unique. SEO writing uses a small number of terms that you will need to understand in order to effectively communicate with clients, peers, and industry leaders. The good news is that we will cover the basics using only the 6 terms below. And most of these terms will probably be familiar to you already.

Consider this a quick reference guide in case you encounter these terms in the future and need a quick refresher.

Internet Browser

Programs used to locate and view web sites. Examples include Firefox, Safari, Chrome, and Explorer.

URL

Website address that appears in the search engine bar. For example, www.proenglishwriters.com and https://proenglishwriters.com/ are both URLs.

Web page

Every single page of content you look at on the internet is a web page. Web pages primarily consist of text, images, and video. A web site generally consists of many individual web pages. So whereas a website (e.g., www.proenglishwriters.com) is akin to a sports team, each web page on the web site corresponds to an individual player on the team. A website consists of a collection of web pages.

Keyword Phrase (also known as 'keyword')

A keyword phrase is simply anything a person searches for on the internet. For example, most people use Google regularly. Every single time you use Google to search for information, you are entering a keyword into Google to find relevant information. Keyword phrases are those words you enter into Google in order to find specific information. Examples of keywords include, 'How to travel from Athens to Santorini?', 'Toronto Maple Leafs', or 'best smart phone'.

Keywords are important in SEO writing. Clients hire writers to create content that enables their websites to appear at the top of google search results (called 'high ranking' websites). In other words, clients are trying to get high ranking in google search results for specific keywords. Note that keywords used in SEO writing is seldom a single word, but much more commonly multiple words or even a short question. This is due to the fact that single words are extremely competitive, and firms often try to specialize in keywords featuring less competition. (these longer keywords are also known as long tail keywords)

What does this mean for SEO writing? The implications are pretty basic. Whatever the keyword you are focusing in your SEO writing, be sure to include it in the title of the article, and use the keyword a couple of additional times within the article. This encourages Google to value your writing in its ranking system, and include in Google search results. A general rule is to use the keyword between 1-2% of the total words in the article. Beware that using the keyword excessively results in negative penalties issued by google, which in turn, makes for unhappy clients. For a 700 word article, using the keyword between 7-9 times is perfect.

Links

Links consist of a group of words you click that bring you to a specific web page. Often, links are underlined and written in blue color. The picture below displays a link (circled in red) that redirects clients to a web page providing additional information concerning the editing of research papers.

Anchor Text

Anchor text is most likely the least familiar term from this list. Keep in mind that the word 'anchor' refers to a heavy weight that is used to keep a ship in one place. In other words, an anchor stabilizes the position of a boat on water.

Anchor text performs a similar idea. Anchor text is the underlined text that you click on in order to visit another web site or web page. An anchor stabilizes a boat, whereas anchor text is the location where websites encourage visitors to take action.

Anchor text and links work in tandem. The link is the method of bringing a visitor to another web site; the anchor text refers to the actual words that the visitor clicks in order to access the link. In the example on the previous page, the link redirects visitors to a web page that delivers information concerning the editing services offered for academic and research papers. The anchor text is "click here for more information", as those are the actual words that the user clicks.

Chapter 5

8 Essential Components to SEO Writing

Remember earlier in the book when I advised you not to worry about difficulties you may have had writing while you were in school? I can still remember my high school teacher talking about thesis statements, topic sentences, and five-paragraph essays; persuasive essays, descriptive essays, and argumentative essays were a headache to try to differentiate.

Well, SEO writing is entirely different. In fact, the format and ideas mentioned above from high school will lead to failure in SEO writing. Therefore, anyone who had writing problems during their school life is in the advantageous position of not have to "unlearn" these concepts.

SEO writing involves writing ideas in a brief manner rather than long-winded paragraphs. It uses simple vocabulary rather than trying to impress teachers by using obscure vocabulary. Brief and simple are the trademarks to SEO writing, and what follows are eight key components for effective SEO writing.

1. *No Long Paragraphs*

Aim for each paragraph to contain 4 sentences or less!

The goal of SEO writing is to make your articles as easy to read as possible. Many readers look at the length of what they are reading before they start, in order to gauge 'how painful' the writing piece will be to read. Long paragraphs are guaranteed to scare off readers, and your clients will not be pleased with your performance.

Remember that people searching the internet are often looking for specific information. Your job is to present information as conveniently as possible. Long paragraphs tend to get skipped by readers who are skimming for information. More often than not, visitors skip long paragraphs, leave your website, and look elsewhere for answers. This is what you are up against in SEO writing.

So aim for paragraphs that contain between 1-4 sentences. White space facilitates a pleasant reading experience, and engages readers far more than pages full of text. Use this to your advantage, and make writing more enjoyable for you in the process.

2. *Use Sub-Headlines to Segment Content*

In conjunction with shorter paragraphs, sub-headlines are an effective method for providing a framework for your content that allow readers to visualize, as well as locate, ideas. In examining this chapter, a quick eye test provides a quick overview of the content you find here. The sub-headlines provide a map for the content in this chapter. This facilitates your ability to locate specific ideas that you are searching for.

Breaking up a larger idea into its components enables for more efficient browsing for information, and a better experience for the user. This represents one of the advantages of the list-style writing that proliferates the web, featuring such headlines as "10 ways to lose weight quickly" or "5 Tips for improving your writing". This format is commonly used on web sites because it is a proven method for delivering content effectively.

3. Use Short Sentences

<u>Sentences should have a maximum of 20 words.</u>

It is important to convey your ideas using short sentences. There are three main reasons for this: First, attention spans for most people today are extremely short. It is important to capture people's attention in a flow of ideas in quick succession in order to keep readers onboard. Second, shorter sentences are typically easier to understand. Furthermore, it ensures that your sentences contain one main idea, and enables readers to successfully follow your train of thought. Lastly, and most importantly, short sentences are preferred by the complex algorithms that dictate search rankings. So using shorter sentences increases the likelihood of your work landing on the first page of Google search results- the ultimate prize in SEO work. There is no better way to keep clients happy, and thus gaining repeat business for yourself, than having your work rank highly on Google searches.

4. *Eliminate Unnecessary Words*

In my many years of editing experience, both in the academic field and in the business world, eliminating the use of unnecessary words is perhaps the most common error in writing. Often when writers are faced with word length requirements, bad habits are developed by adding unnecessary prepositions, extra adjectives, and wordy clauses. While this may seem an effective strategy for meeting client requirements, the resulting lower quality work will harm your reputation as well as your ability to secure repeat business.

When editing your work, consider whether your choice of words adds value to the sentence or paragraph. If it doesn't, then delete it. This is particularly true for longer sentences, as eliminating unnecessary words is often an effective alternative to splitting a longer sentence into two shorter sentences.

5. Use Transitions Regularly

Aim for 30% of sentences to use transitions.

A common theme should be emerging in these SEO components. Transitions, along with using sub-headlines, and short sentences and paragraphs, allow for information to be effectively communicated in a format that readers can easily navigate and understand. Transitions, such as 'first', 'second', and third', as well as 'next' and 'finally', are words that enable a smooth flow of information to be conveyed to readers. They provide signals concerning the flow of content, much like road signs assist travelers in assessing how far they still need to go, or what lies ahead. Importantly, transitions are also used to gauge the writing 'readability' which translates to SEO search rankings. In order to produce high ranking SEO writing, the use of transitions are a required component.

6. Keep Your Writing Simple

Keep in mind that English is not the most common language in the world. In fact, other languages dominate the world in terms of population that use specific languages. So consider there is a good chance that the majority of visitors to web sites, and thus readers of your writing, are not native English speakers.

This means that word use is important. Language is a vehicle for communicating ideas. If someone cannot understand the words you use, then your ideas will not be effectively transferred. Therefore, use simpler words whenever possible. Unlike that high school English class that wanted essays filled with obscure English vocabulary, SEO writing demands that simple (i.e., one- or two- or three- syllable) words be used whenever possible.

7. *Use the Active Voice*

Without getting into the differences between the active and passive voice, the active voice results in shorter sentences that are easier to understand. The active voice follows the pattern of starting with the subject of the sentence followed by the verb and the object. A simple example is 'James purchased a new car.' (Note that the same sentence in the passive voice would read: 'A new car was purchased by James.')

SEO and search engines prefer content that contains less than 10% of sentences using the passive voice, so stick to the active voice. In addition to it being preferred in SEO algorithms, use of the active voice promotes better understanding for readers as well as the use of shorter sentences in your writing.

8. Use Keywords Effectively

As a general rule, keywords can be effectively used by following the steps below:

a. Use the keyword in the Headline of the article

b. Use the keyword in the last Sub-headline in the article

c. Use the keyword in 1-3 other Sub-headlines (depending on the length of the article)

d. Use the keyword in the first sentence (or paragraph) of the article

e. In order to avoid repetition in the article, find synonyms of the keyword and alternate use within the body of the article

These five ideas are not required to be strictly followed. However, they provide effective guidelines for you to get started. Besides, these guidelines make the SEO writing process simpler by eliminating one of the important factors for keeping your clients satisfied- so I'd recommend following these guidelines while starting off. As you develop experience and understanding of what is required in SEO writing, these guidelines will continue to serve as guidance for your writing.

Now that we have outlined the components of SEO writing, I recommend you view the sample article contained in the Appendix. It is 731 words in length, and each of the key components discussed in this chapter are featured.

1. No long paragraphs. Most paragraphs contain between 3-4 sentences.
2. Use of Sub-headlines. The content is divided into 7 distinct sections.
3. Use short sentences. Approximately 4/5 of the sentences in the article contain less than 20 words.

4. Eliminate unnecessary words. After this article was written, it was edited to eliminate words with particular focus on sentences that had more than 20 words.
5. Use of transitions. 46% of the sentences contain a transition word, exceeding the target of 30%.
6. Keep writing simple. The vocabulary and sentence structure was carefully edited for the article.
7. Use the active voice. The article predominantly features the active voice.
8. Use of keywords. The keyword "English essays" accounts for 1.1% of the article, which is between the recommended range of 1-2%.

The article '7 Tips for Writing Amazing English Essays' features a catchy title, and is a good example of the components discussed in this chapter.

Chapter 6

A Writing System that Works

This chapter will outline a writing system for producing high quality content quickly. This proven system is meant to assist someone just starting out in SEO writing. This step-by-step guide will ensure that your first few articles are high quality, which will produce wonderful results and have clients line up for your work.

Step 1- Research

Most of the time, particularly when starting in SEO writing, we will get jobs in which we do not have enough information about the topic in order to write an awesome essay. Therefore, the first step is to use the wonders of technology for locating essay content.

Simply conduct a Google search on the topic. Scan the search results for ideas that you wish to use for your article, and click on whatever seems practical. Take notes on what you find- nothing fancy, just make a list of points on scrap paper (or use the computer of course if you prefer).

Repeat the research steps in the paragraph above until you feel confident that you have collected enough information to write a 700 word article. At this point, organize your notes into a detailed outline. Group related ideas together, and divide each section into brief paragraphs. Separate into headings, and use as much detail as possible. A detailed outline makes the rest of your writing steps much easier! For more details concerning effective outlines, consult www.proenglishwriters.com/make-effective-outlines/.

Whenever you find information that you need to reference, use the link function (hyperlink in MS Word, as shown below) built into your word processor. This includes statistics or ideas from others. If you do reference any information, be sure to note this as you prepare the outline. This helps in keeping all your information tidy, and prevents the inconvenience at the end of your writing job to collect all the references.

How to use Hyperlinks on MS Word.

Highlight what you wish to link, and then click on the Insert tab, and find the hyperlink button as circled in red below.

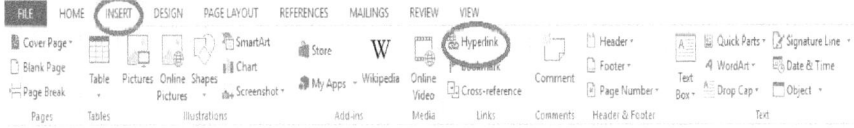

Then simply enter the web address in the 'Address' field with the desired text to be displayed in the "Text to display:" section. (the text will already be filled in if you highlighted the desired text before clicking on the Hyperlink button)

Step 2- Just Write

After you have made your super detailed outline, get comfortable and write your article. While how you choose to do this ultimately depends on your individual style, I recommend strictly following your detailed outline and aiming to complete the rough draft in one sitting. During this step, fix any grammar and spelling errors that are highlighted by your word processor, but mostly leave the editing for later. Instead of interrupting your writing flow, get in a writing groove and concentrate on putting your ideas 'on paper' (well, on the computer screen).

Step 3- Create a Catchy Headline

It is important for you to make your article sound interesting enough to read. If your headline (aka title) does not capture the reader's interest, odds are they will not read your article. Web surfers are inundated with information, and you must learn to somehow grab their attention. Therefore, be sure your article title is catchy and provides a reason for someone to click on it. And of course be sure to include your keyword phrase in the title.

Common article titles use the following formats: 'How to…' '10 Tips for…' or 'Pro Tips on…'. These formats are proven winners in the SEO industry for capturing reader interest- so no need to reinvent the wheel when you are just starting out. Stick with one of these, and spend your time writing quality articles rather than stressing over the headline.

Step 4- Sleep on it

After you have finished your writing and have created a catchy headline, take a break from it. Not only are you mentally tired from all the hard work you have just finished, but your tired mind will play tricks on your ability to identify errors in your writing. If you were to look over your writing in your fatigued state, it is very likely that your brain will subconsciously correct any errors without alerting you consciously to these mistakes.

Allow me to demonstrate. Most of us have seen examples on Facebook, or perhaps through email, of a cute mess of letters in which the reader subconsciously turns garbled text into a meaningful message, such as the following:

It deosn't mttaer in waht oredr the ltteers in a wrod are, the olny iprmoetnt tihng is taht the frist and lsat ltteer be at the rghit pclae. The rset can be a toatl mses and you can sitll raed it wouthit porbelm. Tihs is bcuseae the huamn mnid deos not raed ervey lteter by istlef, but the wrod as a wlohe.

When our writing is fresh in our minds, and we are mentally tired as well, it is likely we will miss errors. In order to build our reputation and to encourage repeat business from clients, we need to make every effort to eliminate errors in our writing (or at least as much as humanly possible). Get some rest, thereby refreshing your mental abilities, and take some time away from your work in order to distance yourself from your writing. After this, you will be better equipped to handle the remaining steps.

Step 5- Edit Your Work, Part I: Spellcheck it

Your word processor has a built-in spellcheck feature. This free tool will identify a lot of errors for you. It makes life easier for you, so be sure to use it. Of course the spellcheck feature isn't perfect- it will identify some 'errors' that aren't actually errors, as well as miss some actual errors in your writing- so be sure to pay close attention.

Step 6- Edit Your Work, Part II: The Eye Test

Editing your work does not mean sipping on coffee, listening to music, and going through your essay. In order to identify errors in your writing, you need to concentrate on what you are doing, and go through your work one word at a time. Eliminate all distractions, and take your time when looking over your work.

Edit your entire document in one sitting if possible. Take care in finding any errors in your work one line at a time. Take a brief break after each longer paragraph, or after completing an entire page of writing. This ensures your mind remains alert.

Once you finish editing your document, I recommend editing a second time following a period of rest. For writers starting out in SEO writing, read the document aloud for your second edit- this will potentially identify errors you have missed using your eyes. Your ears can be a very effective detective, as awkward errors may jump off the page as you read aloud that you may have missed when reading silently.

Step 7- Edit Your Work, Part III: Use an External Expert

You have successfully edited your work. Your eyes and ears have eliminated most, if not all, errors in your writing. Especially when you are just starting out, it is always a good idea to have an external editor look over your work prior to submitting to your client. It somewhat defeats the purpose of writing for money if you end up paying someone to proofread your work, so I recommend using a free tool- www.grammarly.com. (And of course, Pro English Writers will do this for you when you are just starting out.)

This website (www.grammarly.com) offers an 'extra set of eyes and ears' to find any mistakes you may have missed. It only take a few seconds to have your work proofread. The (hopefully) small number of mistakes that are found using this website is well worth the few minutes of your time. Happy clients translate into repeat customers and enhanced reputation.

Step 8- Plagiarism Check

First of all, you will fail at SEO writing (and school, and life) if you steal the ideas and work of others. Clients will undoubtedly pick up on this, and you will not last long in this business. That being said, plagiarism is a concern even if you do not intentionally use the ideas and words of others. If your work resembles another article on the internet by sheer coincidence, a client will treat this transgression with the same furor as a simple copy-and-paste blunder.

In order to check for (unintentional) plagiarism, it is wise to spend the 5 cents on www.copyscape.com for a full review of your writing. In addition to the personal reassurance that results from using this service, it also serves as a quick confirmation that the client will be satisfied with your work. Undoubtedly the client will check your work for plagiarism as well, so it is best for you to proactively test the work yourself before submitting.

Any matches that are identified through Copyscape, whether intentional or not, should be changed. Different word choice will ensure that your content is well received by your client.

If you successfully follow these steps, you will produce amazing content that will wow your clients. These steps provide a process for impressing clients, and for gaining confidence in your ability to write web content in English. When starting off in SEO Writing, follow these steps closely while you determine your own personalized writing system you can employ for success. As you gain experience, confidence, and expand your online portfolio, you will find increased job opportunities available, and be able to command higher rates for your services.

Chapter 7

Build Your Portfolio

You will need to build your portfolio to show prospective clients. These sample articles will serve to add credibility to your ability to produce quality content, and hopefully inspire clients to pay for your work.

Importantly, building your portfolio is also a valuable source of writing experience and feedback. There is no pressure to impress clients with strict deadlines to follow in writing these sample articles. Instead of waiting for a paid job in order to hone your skills and your writing system, choose topics you are familiar with and start now. Concentrate on the process of SEO writing rather than focusing on simply getting paid or completing your job.

It is time to put the ideas contained in this book into action. Follow the steps outlined in chapter 6, which include researching your topic, developing a detailed outline, writing the first draft, creating a catchy headline, editing your work, and conducting a plagiarism test. In spite of you choosing the topic for your first article, pay close attention to each step, and focus on what is really important at every stage.

Before you start writing the article, be sure to consult Chapter 5. The 8 fundamentals included in the chapter are key habits you should start developing in the writing process- not just at the end when you edit your work. Building your portfolio is as much developing your skills and efficiency as it is about creating a collection of materials which will woo your clients.

As a reminder, be sure to write short paragraphs and sentences, use transitions throughout your piece, and write in the active voice using simple vocabulary. Be sure to determine your keyword phrase at the same time you choose your topic (at the very beginning) and use the keyword appropriately (~7-9 times in a 700 word article). And divide your writing into distinct sections, which use sub-headlines to break your article into bite-sized chunks of valuable information.

These sample articles for your portfolio should be about a topic you are already familiar with rather than concerning a topic you think your clients will want to read about. Each writing piece should be about a distinct topic in order to display to clients that you can effectively write articles on a wide range of topics.

There isn't a magic number you should set for your portfolio. Each article you produce represents an opportunity for learning the ropes, and for developing your skills and efficiency. That being said, typically 3-5 articles would suffice as a portfolio to present to clients. If you write more than 5 articles at this stage of developing your skills and portfolio, this allows you to choose those articles you feel are best for inclusion in your portfolio.

As mentioned earlier in the book, an easy way to choose a topic is to consider these phrases:

- How to _____
- X Tips for _____
- The Best _____ for _____

Fill in the blanks with whatever you think makes an interesting title and article! Again, choose what you already have a good understanding of.

I know it can be a bit of a hang up deciding your first topic. You may have doubts and want some reassurance that your topic is suitable. (Don't worry- your topic is fine!) So I have included a list below of potential topics you could choose for your first article.

1. How to Organize Your Closet
2. How to Train Your Cat
3. How to Grow Your Own Basil
4. How to Eliminate Weeds
5. How to Stop Procrastinating
6. How to Plan the Perfect Wedding
7. How to Plan for Early Retirement
8. How to Maximize Your Productivity
9. How to Fall Asleep Fast
10. How to Approach that Cute Girl/Boy
11. The Secret to Finding Your Soul Mate
12. The Truth About Happy Relationships
13. 10 Secrets to Make Studying Easy

14. 7 Tips for Saving Big on Your Next Purchase

15. 7 Tips for Growing Lilies

16. 5 Tips for Glowing Skin

17. 5 Early Signs of Tooth Decay

18. 5 Steps to Finding Your Dream Job

19. 7 Tips to Ace Your Next Job Interview

20. The Most Important Factors for Choosing a Lawyer

21. The Best Way to Find a Mate

22. The Best Ideas for Your Next School Essay

23. The Best Thing to Say on Your Next First Date

24. The Best Place You Will Never Visit

25. The Best Secret Your Mom Never Told You

26. The Best Remedy for Insomnia

27. The Best Cure for Late Night Cravings

28. 10 Medicines You Can Make at Home

29. Quick and Easy Tips for Cleaning Your House

30. The 10 Best Companies to Work For

If you are looking to take advantage of the **free** help offered by Pro English Writers for your initial SEO articles, be sure to choose topics that our readers are interested in. This can include any topic related to writing or English. **These topics all qualify for the free service** offered by Pro English Writers, and examples of suitable topics and articles can be found in the Appendix, as well as posted on the Pro English Writer's website. (https://proenglishwriters.com/community/blog/)

If you wish to write about a different topic= no problem! We are still able to help at very competitive rates. Visit www.proenglishwriters.com for more information.

Chapter 8

Conclusion

Writing web content offers an excellent opportunity to get paid to write online. This provides the freedom to work as much as you wish, whenever and wherever you wish. Getting started in SEO writing takes time in order to establish yourself, gain experience, and develop skills. After putting in the necessary time and effort, you will be positioned to offer more value to clients, and are therefore in a position to charge higher rates for your work.

SEO writing requires very little to get started. This includes the basic technological requirements of access to a computer with internet and a wordprocessor, as well as a paypal account in order to accept payments, and basic English writing skills and the willingness and ability to learn. There is ample opportunity for anyone to reach their personal and financial goals through SEO writing.

SEO writing does not require mastery of the writing skills taught in school. Rather, it involves writing in a specific format that is defined by the method Google utilizes in ranking web pages. While this system is in constant flux, the basic principles described in this book are proven strategies that produce results. As you become experienced in SEO writing, you will be well equipped to recognize, and change with, any Google updates that may change the rules of the game concerning SEO writing.

The purpose of this book is to introduce you to the current opportunity of making money through writing online. We have described the basics for SEO writing, and detailed a proven system for producing quality SEO content. If anyone finds themselves wanting more details concerning the business side of SEO writing, stay tuned for a future book providing ideas on how to develop SEO writing into a freelancing opportunity. Pro English Writers look forward to our continued relationship in your pursuit of personal and professional goals.

In closing, we would like to highlight additional reference materials to help you get started. Found in the Appendix of this book, we present a sample article for you to consult. The hope is that by reviewing the sample SEO article, the practical application of the ideas contained in this book will help guide your success. In addition, be aware that the Pro English Writers website will regularly publish blog posts featuring SEO articles.

(www.proenglishwriters.com/community/blog/)

The next step requires you to take action. Many of the opportunities we are presented with pass us by because we do not act. This book presents an initial step in the journey into SEO writing. Where you end up is entirely dependent on the actions and choices you make. Know that our team at Pro English Writers will accompany you on this journey.

We will give you feedback on your writing, as well as help you get your work published online.

We are committed to your success.

Best Wishes on all your future endeavors.

Sincerely,

Pro English Writers

www.proenglishwriters.com

Appendix

7 Tips for Writing Amazing English Essays

Writing in any language is difficult, and writing stellar English essays is a big challenge. Sometimes, no matter how hard we try, we receive low scores on schoolwork, and produce subpar output at work. However, here are some useful tips for impressing your teachers, and making a good impression at work.

1. Read

Reading English essays is like having your own writing tutor. You learn important tricks and subconsciously process grammar and vocabulary without having to study boring textbooks. Furthermore, reading allows you to move at your own pace, and can be done virtually anywhere and any time.

2. Choose the Right Environment

The key is to create an environment that will enable you to be as productive as possible. A few suggestions include turning off your cell phone during your scheduled writing time, closing your social media sites, turning off anything that makes noise, and sitting in a comfortable chair at a clean table. While you may be inspired to write anywhere you go, in order to produce quality content, you need to set up a work space that maximizes your time and energy.

3. Practice Writing

Producing quality English essays require skills that improve only through use. In order to make writing as exciting as possible, choose a topic you enjoy. Write about a favorite movie, sport, athlete, or anything else you enjoy. In addition, a journal is an excellent way to practice writing about a wide range of topics without feeling like you are 'studying.'

4. Make a Schedule

Life gets busy, and it is often difficult to make time for those tasks that we consider 'optional.' Therefore, it's easy to put off writing while our 'real jobs' (putting kids to bed, washing dishes) take priority. Everyday tasks often fill all of our time available, which results in us never getting started on new projects. After all, the hardest part of everything is getting it started.

So it is important to plan time specifically for writing. If you are currently very busy, waking up earlier may be a practical solution. But not everyone is geared for writing at 6 am. Everyone has a different style, whether you are a night or morning person, or prefer writing in short spurts throughout the day instead of one longer writing period.

In order to determine what works best for you, examine your own schedule and set a time that works best. Once you choose your preferred time, stick with it no matter what and you will find that this time will be something you begin to look forward to every day.

5. Use an Outline

An effective outline serves two purposes. First, it organizes your thoughts, which promotes faster and more efficient writing by not having to worry about 'what comes next' when you write. This results in English essays which readers can easily follow. Also, a framework displaying how each idea fits into 'the big picture' adds a level of clarity and importance to your work.

6. Edit Your Work

Editing your work does not mean sipping on coffee, listening to music, and going through your essay. In order to find errors in your English essays, you need to concentrate on what you are doing, and go through your work word-by-word. So eliminate all distractions, and take your time.

Edit your entire document in one sitting if possible. Take care in finding any errors in your work by carefully editing the article. Once you finish editing your document, edit a second time after a period of rest. For beginning writers, read the essay aloud- this will potentially identify errors you missed with your eyes. Your ears can be a very effective detective, as awkward errors may jump off the page as you read aloud that you may have missed when reading silently.

7. Get Feedback on Your English Essays

Feedback on your writing represents a valuable learning opportunity as you gain insight from the eyes of your readers. Also, it is a good idea to receive feedback from people you admire, professional contacts, paid services, or from clients when you are just beginning.

Writing English essays doesn't have to be difficult. You just need regular practice and determine a writing system that works. But don't worry. If you follow these steps, you will experience a vast improvement in your writing. So don't feel embarrassed about the praise you will receive from teachers and supervisors as you use these tips to improve your writing.

www.ingramcontent.com/pod-product-compliance
Lightning Source LLC
Chambersburg PA
CBHW050237230526
45470CB00005B/1997